PARP!

Brat Packs
PRACTICAL JOKES

Written by Kjartan Poskitt

Hippo

Scholastic Children's Books,
Commonwealth House, 1-19 New Oxford Street
London WC1A 1NU, UK
a division of Scholastic Ltd
London ~ New York ~ Toronto ~ Sydney ~ Auckland

First published by Scholastic Ltd, 1998

Text copyright © Kjartan Poskitt, 1998
Illustrations copyright © Martin Chatterton, 1998

ISBN 0 590 19799 1

Printed by Cox & Wyman Ltd, Reading, Berks.

Contents:

PRACTICAL JOKES

Welcome to the powerful world of practical jokes. Practical jokes are a great way to have a laugh with your friends, and if necessary bring somebody down a peg or two.

You'll have already noticed you get two free things with this book, and you'll find out what to do with them later. You'll also need a few more bits and pieces which you should be able to find easily, but the most important thing you'll need is ... A VICTIM!

Before you play any practical joke, you must carefully consider your victim. If the victim is going to be one of your friends, you must be sure that they will think it funny afterwards – because if they don't then you could suddenly be very unpopular! Sometimes, there are occasions when you need to play a practical joke for REVENGE. This is especially effective if somebody is really stuck up, or always jumping queues or spreading nasty stories about people – if you can make them look stupid in front of everybody then you are mighty indeed.

To make sure your practical jokes are successful, you'll probably need to practise them a lot … or else you might find the joke will be on you!

Joke ratings

Some jokes in this book are fine to play on almost anybody, but others are a bit diabolical. To help you decide, each joke has a diabolicalness rating. Look out for the following symbols:

Just a bit diabolical:

Fairly diabolical:

Diabolically diabolical:

Some jokes might also need a bit of help from a friendly adult, and these are marked:

Spiders at large

The main thing any joker needs comes with this book – a plastic spider! You can get much bigger ones, but they never look realistic and their use is limited. With a bit of thought you will get far more fun from this one.

The secret of plastic spiders (or rubber worms or flies or mice for that matter) is where you put them. If you put your spider in the middle of a table then shout, 'Ooh look! A spider!', you won't get much of a reaction. What you need to do is leave the spider some place where people won't expect to find it – and certainly won't want to find it! Here are some ideas:

🕷 **On the little handle at the end of the string for the bathroom light switch.**

🕷 **Inside your sister's face powder box.**

🕷 **Under the soap in the shower.**

🕷 Folded into a tissue, then tucked neatly back into the box.

🕷 Tucked into a toilet roll.

🕷 In a cereal packet.

🕷 Inside a margarine tub. You can also use marmalade jars, or pop the spider under the lid of a butter or cheese dish if your family uses them. Of course if you put the spider anywhere near food, be sure to give it a good wash first.

🕷 In the end of a sock or pair of tights that somebody is going to put on.

🕷 In an ice cube! Buy yourself a really small fake spider and put it in the ice cube tray, fill it with water and freeze it. (Mind you, make sure that the person getting the ice cube sees the spider before they swallow it.)

🕷 Dangling on a thread outside somebody's bedroom door. When they open the door all bleary-eyed in the morning, they'll walk into the spider! Especially effective for teenage brothers and sisters (although you might not get your spider back).

You can also have fun if you tie a very thin thread to your spider. If you're eating somewhere with a white table or tablecloth, get a white thread and tie it carefully to the end of one of the spider's front legs. Hide the spider under the edge of a plate that your victim is using.

When the plate is picked up, pull the thread so the spider seems to scuttle along the table. It's guaranteed to make them jump!

Another good spider joke is to have the spider sitting on your shoulder. (This is even better if you have a thread attached to it so you can make it twitch slightly.) When somebody notices the spider and tells you, grab it with your hand and say, 'Mmm, I love spiders!' then pretend to put it in your mouth!

You can probably think of lots of other things to do with your spider but there's just one warning – a few people are ARACHNOPHOBIC. This means that they are really terrified of spiders, even plastic ones, and any spider joke you play on them honestly won't be funny. It's better all round if you find a different joke to play on them.

The plate lifter

You are probably wondering what the thing with a squeezy bit and tube is that came with this book, aren't you? To be accurate, it is known as a 'plate lifter', but for a good joker it has lots of other important uses.

There are three bits to the plate lifter, there's the bulb, the tube and the plate lifter. You'll need to straighten the tube by pulling it taut lots of times.

The plate lifter gives some very spooky effects if you set it up right, although plate lifting isn't the best one! Later in this book you'll find how it can bring nasty things to life, but first, here are some other good tricks.

The haunted glass

It pays to practise this trick before you try it.

You need a tall plastic glass, and for the best effect have a couple of spoons sticking out of it to make it rattle. Put the plate lifter on a table and run the tube off to the edge.

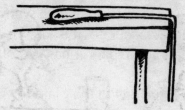

Cover the plate lifter and tube with a piece of paper to hide it, then carefully position the glass over it.

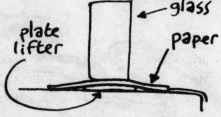

Secretly hold the bulb in your hand. You should find that by squeezing the bulb, you can make the glass wobble, and by giving a few quick pushes it might even fall over. (Make sure it won't do any damage!)

When your victim is in the room, set the glass rocking. With a bit of luck your victim will notice the glass moving before you have to point it out.

If you pretend to be surprised too, they could start getting quite worried!

The wobbly cup

The plate lifter also works well when people are using cups and saucers. If you put the plate lifter under the saucer and give it a quick flick, the cup may well fall over in the saucer with a good clatter. Very spooky!

Hello spider!

This is a really freaky joke using both your spider and your plate lifter!

1. Tip the sugar out of a sugar bowl.

2. Put a little block, like a toy building brick, in the bottom of the bowl. Put the plate lifter on top of the block and neatly run the tube out of the bowl and off the edge of the table.

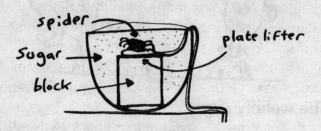

3. Put your spider on the plate lifter.

4. Carefully put the sugar back in the bowl so that it comes up to the level of the block and so that it just covers the spider.

5. When your victim is looking at the sugar bowl, give the bulb a few squeezes. The spider will seem to dig itself out of the sugar. YUCK!

The secret squirter

If you want you can convert your lifter to a secret squirter! Very neatly remove the lifter bit by cutting through the tube with a pair of scissors. You should leave at least 3 cm of tube still attached to the lifter if you want to use it again. You are then left with the joker's favourite weapon – the secret squirter!

Special note: If you want to go back to using your squirter as a plate lifter, you can fix the two ends of the tube back together with sellotape. You only need to wrap the sellotape round a couple of times, but make sure you do it very tightly!

What you need to do:

1. Run some water into a basin.

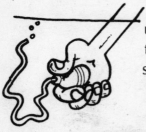

2. Hold the bulb and tube under the water and squeeze the bulb a few times until air stops coming out of the tube. Your squirter is now loaded!

3. Take the bulb and tube out of the basin, and point the tube somewhere safe.

4. Give the bulb a good hard squeeze. Pretty good, eh?

Now you've got your secret squirter, you can plan all sorts of evil places to use it. You should find that once you've filled it with water, if you're careful, you can carry it round without the water coming out until you want it to.

Whale impressions

This joke might make you a little bit wet yourself, but it will have people in fits of laughter! You need to wear a head band or a baseball cap, and stick the tube of the squirter up the back so it points up at the back of your head.

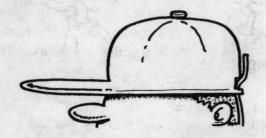

Tell people you can do an impression of a whale coming up for air. Of course they won't believe you, so just squeeze the bulb and water will shoot out of the top of your head!

Secret water pistol

If there's somebody who needs cooling down a bit, but you don't want to be caught doing it, all you need to do is fix the end of the tube under the brim of a baseball cap, and then run it down behind your back. As long as the victim isn't looking directly at you when you squirt, they'll never realize who did it!

The spitting spider

Put your spider on a table and secretly run the squirter tube underneath it. You can use a bit of blu-tack to hold the squirter in place. Tell your victim you've got a spitting spider. When they laugh and say, 'Don't be stupid, it's only plastic!' blast them!

Sea shells

You know those funny hollow shells people find on the beach – they hold them to their ear and say, 'I can hear the sea'? Well here's a good joke to play:

Get a funny looking shell and fix up the tube of your squirter inside it. Hold the shell to your ear and tell your victim you can hear the sea. Ask if they want to hear the sea and hold the shell to their ear. Then you squirt water in their ear and say, 'Whoops! The tide's coming in!'

The scorpion letter

Here's a super joke which always gets a big laugh. Your victim gets a letter from 'The Institute of Tropical Insects'. When the envelope is opened something very nasty starts thrashing about inside – a real shocker!

<u>You will need:</u>

- a piece of writing paper (which feels slightly thicker than normal paper)
- an envelope
- a bit of sticky tape
- two thin elastic bands
- a piece of stiff wire about 20 cm long (a bit of old wire coat hanger is ideal)
- a metal ring about 3 cm across. You can use a thin washer, or an empty keyring, or make one with a bit more wire.

<u>What you need to do:</u>

1. First bend the long bit of wire like this:

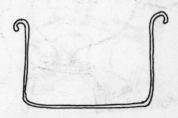

21

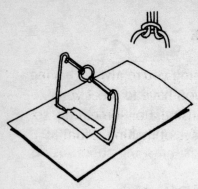

2. Fix the wire ring on to it with the elastic bands and then tape the whole thing onto the sheet of writing paper.

3. Turn the ring round lots and lots of times until the elastic bands get nice and tight, then fold the paper over it like this:

4. Finally put the folded paper in the envelope, pass it to somebody and wait for the fun!

Freaky handshakes

Shaking hands is something you're always having to do, especially when you have to meet your long lost cousins from Australia or something, so here are some simple ways of making it fun.

The wet handshake

Here's one to baffle your victim! You need to use your squirter bulb and the tube. Fill the squirter with water, then carefully run the tube down your sleeve so it pokes out at your wrist. If you have a watch, you can hold it in place by tucking the nozzle under the strap.

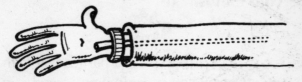

When you shake hands, secretly squeeze the squirter with your other hand. With a bit of practise, you should be able to keep your hand dry, but the victim's hand will be all wet!

The dead handshake

This must be the simplest joke in this book, but also one of the most effective. As you reach out to shake hands, just let your hand go completely limp. When the person gives you a funny look, explain that your hand is dead!

This handshake is even more freaky if you combine it with...

The cold handshake

This is a perfect joke to play at parties where there are ice cubes you can use. Hold an ice cube in your hand for as long as you can. (Be careful where the drips of water go. It might be sensible to hold the ice cube over a glass.) When you think your hand is really cold, quickly dry it on a cloth and then as soon as you can shake hands with somebody.

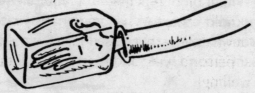

The snotty handshake

If you have to shake hands with somebody you really don't like, here's what to do. Smile pleasantly, then just as you are reaching out your hand, suddenly pretend to sneeze, bringing your hand up to cover your nose. Still smiling, hold your hand out again.

If you want to make this handshake REALLY nasty, you need a little more preparation. Get a grape and take the skin off, then squish it into the palm of your hand. A bit of mushed up banana is also good, or even a bit of jelly. If you keep your hand half closed while you do your pretend sneeze, it will hide the thing from your victim and help you hold onto it. When you finally reach out, splat whatever you've used into the palm of the other person's hand and most important of all – keep smiling!

The three cups

Not everybody wants to be squirted with water or attacked by spiders, so here's a nice joke which everybody will like. You need three paper cups that look exactly the same.

Put the cups on a table in a line with the middle one facing down, like this:

The aim of this trick is to make all the cups face downwards. But there are three rules you have to follow in the process:

🐜 **You have to turn over TWO cups every turn.**

🐜 **You must do it in THREE turns, no more or less.**

🐜 **You must turn each cup at least once.**

You show everybody how easy this is to do...
Turn over cups 1 and 2, then cups 1 and 3, then cups 1 and 2. Easy!

You even set the cups up again and do it once more to show how easy it is ... but for fun you do it a different way! (Actually this will confuse them.)

Turn over cups 2 and 3, then cups 1 and 3, then cups 2 and 3. What could be simpler?

It's their turn ... so you set up the cups for them, but they will never be able to do the trick!

Why? Because when it's their turn you set the cups up like this...

Unless they are VERY observant and realize what you've done, they will never manage to get all three cups facing down!

(By the way, this trick works best with cups, but you could use three coins the same, and lay them out heads, tails, heads, and ask people to make them all tails.)

Raspberry shocker

This is a brilliant joke to play on somebody who is GREEDY!

One nice day when you're having raspberries, wait till your victim has eaten a few. You then say, 'Did those raspberries taste all right to you?' Next you take a raspberry and break it open and say, 'Because this one's full of maggots!' Your victim will choke at seeing lots of white grubby things in your raspberry!

What you need are some grains of rice, which you carefully push inside a raspberry. Make sure you know which raspberry you've doctored, then at the right moment, open it up!

With a bit of preparation, you can make this even more spooky using a tomato and your plate lifter. (You might even manage it with a big strawberry.)

What you need to do:

1. Cut the top off the tomato, then scoop out the insides with a teaspoon.

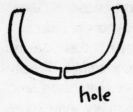

hole

2. Very carefully, make a little hole in the bottom of the tomato.

3. Carefully fold the plate lifter together so you can squeeze it through the hole, then unfold it inside the tomato. Cover the plate lifter with rice!

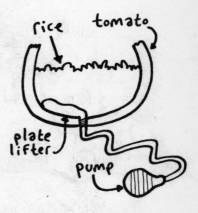

rice   tomato

plate lifter

pump

When you show the tomato to your greedy victim, work the lifter a bit and your rice will look like heaving maggots!

Phantom noises

If you're allowed to use a tape recorder, then here's a great way of spooking people. You'll also need a blank cassette tape, preferably at least a C60.

Fast forward the tape almost to the end. Then record whatever spooky noises you like! Just a scratching sound is quite effective, otherwise you might want to put on some evil chuckles or just shout BOO! The best sounds are quite short, and after you've left a gap, you can make some more.

The secret of this joke is to pick your time to play it. Maybe your mum likes to have a quiet read in the evening, or your brother needs silence to do some homework. As long as there's a time when the room will be quiet for a while, you can play the joke.

All you do is rewind the cassette back to the beginning, then secretly push the play button (it might be clever to do this before the person enters the room). It's best if you leave the room too, so that your victim won't see you laughing.

What happens is that when your victim is nicely settled and all is quiet, suddenly your spooky noises start coming from nowhere! Because nobody has been near the tape recorder, they won't realize where the sounds are coming from, especially if you have kept them short.

The sliced banana

Your victim peels a banana and to their amazement inside it is already cut into slices!

Preparing the trick banana takes a bit of care, and should be done just before you play the joke or it might all go brown and horrid.

You need to get a long pin, and stick it carefully into the side of the banana.

Wiggle it backwards and forwards, pushing the edge of the pin through the banana inside, and so slicing through it.

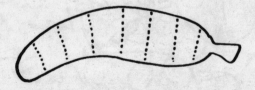

Do this a few times along the banana to make more slices.

Living sweets

Here's a joke that makes offering a bag of sweets around more fun.

<u>What you need to do:</u>

1. Paint your middle finger the same colour as one of the sweets.

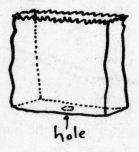

hole

2. Make a small hole in the bottom of the bag.

3. Hold the bag in your hand, but with your painted finger sticking up inside the bag.

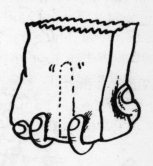

4. Offer the sweets, but wiggle your finger as someone puts their hand in!

The sweet gnome

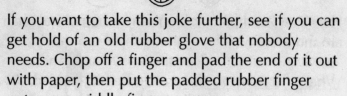

If you want to take this joke further, see if you can get hold of an old rubber glove that nobody needs. Chop off a finger and pad the end of it out with paper, then put the padded rubber finger onto your middle finger.

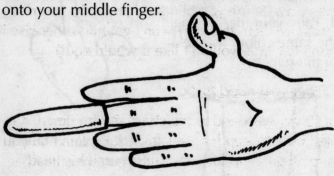

You can draw some eyes on it, and even stick on some cotton wool hair! Put your finger in the bag as before and hide the 'gnome' under some sweets. When your victim reaches into the packet, make the 'gnome' suddenly sit up!

The big leap

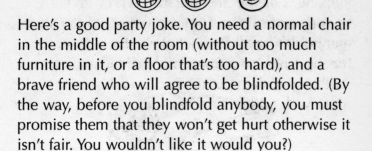

Here's a good party joke. You need a normal chair in the middle of the room (without too much furniture in it, or a floor that's too hard), and a brave friend who will agree to be blindfolded. (By the way, before you blindfold anybody, you must promise them that they won't get hurt otherwise it isn't fair. You wouldn't like it would you?)

<u>What you need to do:</u>

1. Lead the friend to the chair, sit him down, and tell him to keep his arms folded. Explain that you are all going to lift the chair up until his head touches the ceiling.

2. One of your friends needs to have a book with a hard cover, and you need to get down on the floor.

3. Your other friends must hold the seat or legs of the chair and lift it up so that the victim's feet are only just above the floor. (Your lifting friends must be very quiet, and also make sure they don't come into contact with the victim.)

4. You shout out, 'Can you feel the ceiling yet?' Because you are lying on the floor, the victim will think he is high in the air! The friend with the book then gently touches the book onto the top of the victim's head. The victim will be convinced that his head has touched the ceiling!

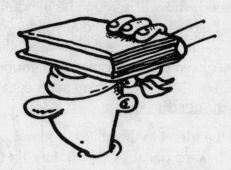

5. You suddenly start panicking! You shout, 'Be careful! They can't hold you up! Quick, you've got to jump off!'

6. Your victim will do a massive leap – and be amazed that the floor is right under his feet!

The egg walk

Here's another great party joke.

<u>What you need to do:</u>

1. Clear as much floor space as you can and then get two or three friends to stand by the door.

2. Let them see you put some eggs around the empty floor. They have to remember eggs-actly where the eggs are!

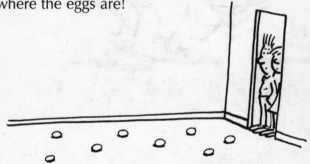

3. Ask your friends to leave the room and while they are outside they have to put on blindfolds!

4. PICK ALL THE EGGS UP! (And put them away safely.)

5. Let your blindfolded friends into the room. Say there's a prize for the first one to walk across the room without breaking any eggs!

Of course you'll have a great laugh watching them tiptoeing very nervously across the empty floor!

Food colouring

There are tons of jokes you can do using food colouring. You can find it in the supermarket next to all the baking things, it comes in little bottles and doesn't cost much. Blue is usually the best colour, but of course you can choose your favourite.

Mouldy bread

Remember to always wash your hands and be very tidy when playing with food!

Here's a real breakfast time shocker! If you have sliced bread, carefully open up a packet and then put just one or two small drops of colour on one or two slices in the middle. Put the bread all back in the packet and wait until somebody gets down to the 'mouldy' slices. When they get all fussy, you can offer to eat them!

If you have unsliced loaves of bread, it's even better. Turn the loaf upside down and make a tiny hole in the bottom with the end of a teaspoon. Drop just one or two drops of colour into the hole. Put the bread the right way up and wait until somebody cuts into it and finds the 'mould'!

The horrid shower

If you have a shower in your house then you might be able to play a brilliant joke, although you'll definitely need a friendly adult to help with this one!

Ask your friendly adult to see if the nozzle of the shower will undo from the tube. If it does, pour a bit of food colouring into the tube so that it sits in the bit that dangles down. Then get your adult to fix the shower nozzle back on.

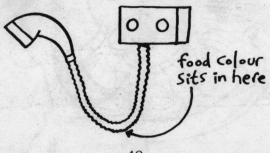

food colour sits in here

When somebody goes in to use the shower ... listen out for the scream!

Funny food

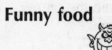

Because food colouring isn't at all poisonous, it is quite safe to put in cooking. If you are having visitors for tea, you can have some real fun by asking whoever is doing the cooking to make the food the wrong colour. White things like potatoes are brilliant if you add some food colour to them, and your visitors will be really shocked!

The corner caper

You need a friend to help you with this joke. You also need a piece of string at least 3 m long, and a bit of chalk.

<u>What you need to do:</u>

1. On the outside of a building put a little chalk mark on the wall about 1½m in from the corner.

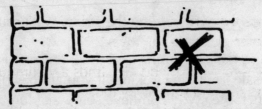

2. Get your friend to hold the piece of string up to the chalk mark.

3. Take the other end of the string round the corner, and put a chalk mark on the wall where the end of the string comes to.

4. When a suitable victim comes past, ask if they would be kind enough to help you. All they need to do is hold the string to the chalk mark for a few seconds while you finish some measuring.

5. When they are holding the string, walk round the corner and then run away!

6. Of course your friend also finds a victim just like you did and runs away too.

   The victims could be standing there holding the string for ages!

Cracked mirror

If you can find a bar of soap that is worn right down to the last little bit, there's a good joke to play. Make sure the soap is dry so that there is a thin hard edge, a bit like a small coin.

Using the edge of the soap, carefully draw a few 'crack' lines across the corner of a mirror. It's best if the lines are fairly straight, and if you have two or three coming from the same point. Carefully flick off any extra crumbly bits of soap with a bit of toilet paper.

Stand back and have a look – if you've got it right the mirror will seem to be cracked! This illusion works better if the room isn't too bright.

Springers

These will give somebody a jump!

You'll need a strong elastic band and two small lolly sticks, or short bits of pencil. Wrap the elastic band round the two sticks a few times so that they are loosely joined together.

Wind the springer up by twiddling one of the sticks round until the elastic band gets really tight. If you drop it, you'll see it springs round and goes mental.

You can now think of some places to put your springer. How about under some socks in a drawer, or in a cornflake packet?

45

Horror hand

Here's a really nasty illusion, bound to give anybody a real shock!

<u>You need:</u>

✴ **bandages**

✴ **a bit of cardboard (about 8x4 cm)**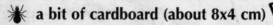

✴ **a small fat wood screw**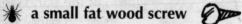

✴ **some red paint.**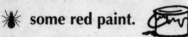

Be careful because the point of the screw might be sharp.

<u>What you need to do:</u>

1. Bend the cardboard down the middle, then stick the screw through one half.

Fold the cardboard over so that the other half covers the head of the screw.

2. Hold the cardboard against the back of your hand so that the screw sticks out, then wrap the bandage round your hand so that it holds the cardboard in place.

3. Make the screw poke through the bandage. Paint on some red blood, or put on a dab of tomato sauce.

4. Clutch your hand and make some moaning noises – when anybody asks what the matter is, suddenly show them the back of your hand!

Teeth smash

Here's a real shocker which will scare people at first, but then they should get a big laugh! You need some white peppermints broken in half. (You could do this in your mouth of course.)

<u>What you need to do:</u>

1. Secretly slip the mints into your mouth as you are leaving a room.

2. 'Accidentally' walk into the edge of the door. (If you give the bottom of the door a kick as you do this, it will look very realistic!)

3. Grab your mouth and say, 'I think I've broken all my teeth!'

At first nobody will believe you but...
    Let a few bits of mint come out of your mouth
… then a few more … then a few more!

If you think your victims are tough enough, and
your taste buds can stand it, have a spoonful of
tomato sauce in your mouth as well as the mints!

All night long

This joke works amazingly well in the summer months. You'll need some black dustbin bags, and probably a friendly adult to help you.

Open up the dustbin bags into large black sheets. One evening when your victim has gone to bed, fix the black sheets over their bedroom window so that no daylight will get in next morning. If you can arrange to stop their alarm clock from ringing, that's even better.

When the victim wakes up, they will still think it is dark outside, and go back to sleep. If you're really successful they might miss a whole day out!

The shaky book

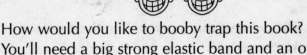

How would you like to booby trap this book? You'll need a big strong elastic band and an old battery.

Open the book up about in the middle then put the elastic band round the back pages. Tuck the battery between the elastic band and the back cover, then twist it round so that the elastic band holds it.

Keep twisting the battery until it feels fully wound up. Carefully put the book down so that it is lying on the battery, and not letting the battery unwind itself.

Say to a victim, 'Have you seen this absolutely brilliant book?'

When they pick the book up ... eeek!

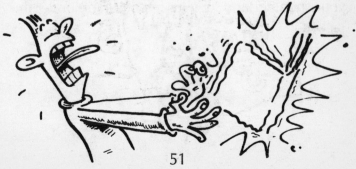

The phantom hand

This joke is especially brilliant if you're going to a fancy dress party.

You go up to your victims looking quite normal. You smile, say hello, even shake hands, then suddenly clutch your stomach. Just as they are wondering what the matter is, out of your shirt bursts a horrible hand which can reach round and grab them. It might even grab your neck and start throttling you!

Good one, eh?

You will need some sort of jacket and a loose shirt to wear. Get some old newspaper, stuff it down the left sleeve of the jacket, and stick the end of the sleeve in the pocket.

sleeve packed with newspaper

When you put the jacket on, don't put your arm in the stuffed sleeve, just let the jacket rest on your shoulder and let your left arm hide under the jacket.

Arrange the dummy arm so it looks like you've got your left hand in your jacket pocket. The best way to check this is to put your right hand in your other pocket and check in a mirror to see if they both look about the same.

When you're happy with how it looks, carefully take the jacket off again.

Next you need to make your left arm look really horrible. Use face paints to paint your hand and arm green, right down to your elbow. Next you can stick black tape over your finger nails to make them look really nasty.

open button

When the paint is absolutely dry, put the baggy shirt on, but don't put your left arm into the sleeve, keep it hidden inside the shirt across your stomach. Leave a button undone in the middle so you will be able to quickly poke your arm through.

Finally put the jacket on with the false arm in place, and you're ready!

When it's time for the phantom hand to pop out, clutch your stomach with your right hand, and then shove your left hand through the gap in your shirt.

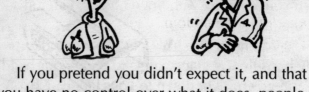

If you pretend you didn't expect it, and that you have no control over what it does, people will get a real shock!

Of course, if you have a good glove puppet, you could put that on your hand instead of making it look horrible.

The severed finger

No joke book is complete without this great trick. You need a matchbox, some cotton wool and some red paint.

<u>What you need to do:</u>

1. Cut a slot in the bottom of the outer sleeve of the matchbox.

2. Cut a hole at one end of the bottom of the matchbox tray.

3. Put some cotton wool on the bottom of the tray.

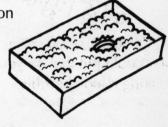

4. Stick your finger through the hole and lie it down on the cotton wool. Put a bit more cotton wool round the back of your finger.

5. Paint some red round your finger, especially where it comes through the hole in the tray. Splash a bit onto the cotton wool too.

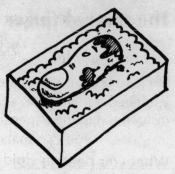

6. Slide the outer sleeve of the match box over your finger, then hold the matchbox with your other fingers.

7. Tell your victim that you've found a severed finger – then open the matchbox and show them. While they are looking, wiggle your finger!

56

Some simple jokes

Itching powder

Instead of buying expensive itching powder from joke shops, you can make your own quite easily. All you need is some old bread that has dried out and gone hard. Break it up into little crumbs, and then store it in a matchbox! It's amazing how effective tipping some of your 'itching powder' into somebody's sock can be!

Rude noises

Get a balloon and blow it up, but don't tie a knot. Pinch the neck of the balloon on both sides and pull it apart.

You will find you can make a wide range of noises, most of which sound rude! If you secretly do this while everybody is distracted by watching telly or something, you can then look round crossly and say, 'Was that you?'

Paper snow

Tear up some paper into little bits, put it in an umbrella and then close the umbrella up. When the victim opens the umbrella, they will think it's snowing!

Another umbrella trick is to get about 50 cm of thread, tie one end to your spider and the other end to one of the struts inside the umbrella. When

the victim opens the umbrella, your spider will
jump out and dangle in front of them!

Ink puddle

Get a nice new shiny black plastic bin liner, find
a bit that is completely flat and has no creases,
then cut a puddle shape out of it.

Put the 'puddle' on a clean table and leave a
pen on top of it. Shout to your victim that your
pen has just leaked all over the table. When they
come and see it, they will get a shock!

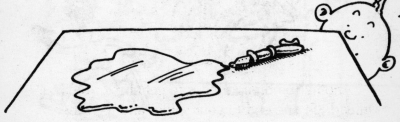

Pillar box prison

You can get the most amazing reactions by pretending somebody is stuck inside a pillar box. When you see a victim approaching, pretend you haven't seen them, but start talking into the letter hole and say things like, 'How did you get in there?', 'No, I can't see your mummy anywhere', 'I don't know if the police have keys to get you out' and 'Stay there, I'll go and get help.' Just as the victim approaches, rush off looking worried, shouting, 'I'll be back!' If you do it right, after you've gone the victim will start talking into the pillar box too!

The caught thread

Here's one that works an absolute treat on anybody who has a favourite woolly jumper or cardigan.

Get a long piece of wool roughly the same colour as the jumper. At the end of the wool tie a little hook – you could make one out of a paper clip.

When your victim goes past, quickly and gently hook the piece of wool onto the back of their jumper.

Wait until they've gone right past then say, 'Oh dear, your jumper's all coming unravelled at the back!'

When they look round and see the long thread they'll get a nasty shock!

Worms

If you ever have spaghetti for tea and there is some left over, put it in a bag and keep it! There are lots of funny places to put your 'worms' especially if you use your plate lifter too.

<u>What you need to do:</u>

1. Find a victim that keeps a pot plant. Put the plate lifter on top of the soil and cover it with a few 'worms'.

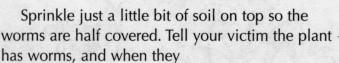

Sprinkle just a little bit of soil on top so the worms are half covered. Tell your victim the plant has worms, and when they look to see, just squeeze the lifter bulb a few times, and the worms will look alive!

2. Hide a long piece of spaghetti in the palm of your hand while you are holding an apple. Bite into the apple, then suddenly say, 'Oh no! I've got a worm in my apple!' Slowly pull the spaghetti from your hand, as if you were pulling it out of the apple.

A final word of warning...

Victims of practical jokes will react in one of three different ways.

1. They will have a good laugh with you. These are the best people, and it also means you've picked a good joke to play.

2. They will get very cross and upset and cause you grief. If it is a friend, then you've played the wrong joke on them and you'll have to apologize. However if it is somebody horrid who needed teaching a lesson, then good for you.

3. They won't either laugh or get upset, instead they will just stare at you very quietly. If this happens, then BE VERY AFRAID INDEED ... because this sort of person is already planning a diabolical joke to play on you in revenge!